Sent by Jesus

Simon Cansdale

Series Editor: James Jones

Illustrated by Taffy

The Bible Reading Fellowship

Published by
The Bible Reading Fellowship
Peter's Way
Sandy Lane West
Oxford
OX4 5HG
ISBN 0 7459 2577 4
Albatross Books Pty Ltd
PO Box 320
Sutherland
NSW 2232
Australia
ISBN 0 7324 0814 8

First edition 1995
10 9 8 7 6 5 4 3 2 1 0

Acknowledgments
Scriptures quoted from the Good News Bible
published by The Bible Societies/HarperCollins
Publishers Ltd., UK © American Bible Society, 1966,
1971, 1976, 1992, with permission.

A catalogue record for this book is available
from the British Library

Printed and bound in Malta

Contents

1 Stephen fol

Think about how many people you've seen killed. Shot, run over, ripped apart, eaten . . . all on television, of course. It's easy to see so many that you forget that each day people are killed and injured in terrifying ways. (The average 14-year-old has seen 18,000 people murdered on TV).

The book of Acts in the New Testament is the story of what happened to the first followers of Jesus after he came back to life. Some of them were killed, and nearly all of them were beaten up. They learnt that this is sometimes part of following Jesus.

Jesus promised that the disciples would carry on the work he had started. They shouldn't be surprised if people treated them as badly as he was treated. To help them, they would receive the Holy Spirit, which was like having him with them all the time.

One of the first stories in Acts is about a man called Stephen. One of his jobs in the Church was to give out food to those who didn't have enough (Acts 6:2–5). Stephen was arrested. They accused him of things he'd never done. When he refused to turn his back on Jesus, the high priest and Council who were questioning him went mad . . .

Read Acts 7:57–8:1

With a loud cry the members of the Council covered their ears with their hands. Then they all rushed at him at once, threw him out of the city, and stoned him. The witnesses left their cloaks in the care of a young man named Saul. They kept on stoning Stephen as he called out to the Lord, 'Lord Jesus, receive my Spirit!' He knelt down and cried out in a loud voice, 'Lord! Do not remember this sin against them!' He said this and died. And Saul approved of his murder.

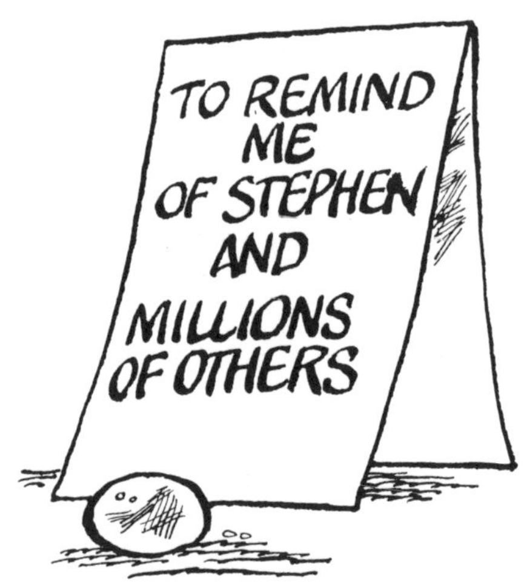
TO REMIND
ME
OF STEPHEN
AND
MILLIONS
OF OTHERS

lows Jesus

Stephen didn't hold back when following Jesus started to look dangerous. In fact, there's something very familiar about the way he died. Here's what he said . . .

"Lord Jesus, receive my Spirit.

farther! in you hands Place my Spirit

Lord! Do not remember this sin against them.

"Forgive them, farther! hey dont know What theys are doing"!

Jesus said similar things as he was put to death. Look up these two verses in Luke's Gospel and compare them with what Stephen said; Luke 23:34 and Luke 23:46. Write the matching verse under Stephen's words.

Stephen shows two crucial things about following Jesus.

The first is faith. Even as he dies, facing a roaring crowd alone, he trusts Jesus. He knew that death would not be the end because Jesus had come through it. Having this faith in Jesus allows us to stare even our own death in the face, and know that Jesus can bring us through it.

The second is forgiveness. Following Jesus encouraged Stephen to forgive the people who savagely pelted him with rocks. He could do this because Jesus had forgiven him for everything and because he knew that Jesus did the same when he was killed. Following Jesus means forgiving even the people that cause us terrible pain. This is hard, but Jesus showed that this is the way God treats people.

There are many Christians throughout the world today who face the same dangers as Stephen. They are tortured, kept in prisons and killed for following Jesus.

Look for a stone that you can easily hold in your hand. Keep it in your room as a reminder of Christians who are suffering like Stephen. When you see it, pick it up, pray for them and pray for the ones persecuting them.

Heavenly Father, thank you that Stephen trusted in you even as he died. I pray for Christians around the world who are suffering because they're following you. Please give them faith to trust in you, and forgiveness for the people who are hurting them. Please change the hearts of their persecutors. Amen.

2

As Stephen was murdered, a mysterious young man called Saul watched with approval. He was like a coach at a football match in which the team on the other side had only one player. Holding the team's tracksuits, he watched them thrash the one-player team. Goal after goal rained in. He didn't stop the game, or rush on to say it was unfair—he watched with satisfaction.

Who was this man? Why was he so pleased to see Stephen killed? Why was he there in the first place? To find out, you need to go on something of a detective hunt, looking through statements that Saul made and letters that he wrote. You'll find them all in the New Testament.

Home Town?
(Acts 21:39) Tarusus.in.Cilicia

Citizen of which superpower?
(Acts 22:27) Roman..citizen

Member of which tribe?
(Philippians 3:5) Benjamin...

Trained by?
(Acts 22:3) Gamaliel.........

Father's sect?
(Acts 23:6) Pharisees.........

Ability to keep the Jewish law?
(Philippians 3:6)
☐ Poor ☐ Average ☑ Very Good

Attitude to Christians? (Acts 26:11)
☐ Best mates ☑ Hunted them down
☐ 'What's a Christian?'

Saul hated Christians for what he thought were very respectable reasons. It's not that they had killed his best friend or stolen something from him. They shocked him by what they said about Jesus. Saul was one of the most deeply religious people of his day. He was totally committed to God. But he could not accept that the Messiah, the one who was to save Israel, could be some wandering preacher from the backwaters of Galilee who ended up dying as a common criminal.

The fact that he ended up dying as a common criminal was the surest proof for Saul that Jesus was a nobody. Now some of his followers were saying that he was alive again. Worse, that to be forgiven for your sins you just had to believe in him to accept God's forgiveness. That was totally outrageous! It turned upside down everything that Saul believed in. That's why he hunted down the first Christians—he thought that they were cooking up new and very wrong ideas about God. He had to silence them before more people believed their dangerous stories.

There are many different reasons why people beat up, imprison or kill Christians today. Jesus' attitude to these people is clear:

2 Who is this man?

Read Matthew 5:44

> *'Love your enemies and pray for those who persecute you.'*

Here is a prayer for people who are persecuting Christians. Use it now.

Almighty Father, you know all the people in the world who hate and hurt Christians. You know why they are so hard-hearted. Please forgive them. Please stop them being so violent. Show them your love. I pray that they will become followers of Jesus. Amen.

Talk to your youth leader or minister about spending time in one of your meetings or services praying for persecuted Christians around the world, and the people persecuting them.

For more information about persecuted Christians, write to:

Keston Research, PO Box 276,
Oxford OX2 6BF

IISIC, St Andrew's Centre,
St Andrew's Rd, Plaistow,
London E13

Saul in action

Stephen died handing over his life to Jesus; Saul lived on to make sure that Jesus was never spoken of again:

3

Read Acts 8:1–4

> *That very day the church in Jerusalem began to suffer cruel persecution. All the believers, except the apostles, were scattered throughout the provinces of Judea and Samaria. Some devout men buried Stephen, mourning for him with loud cries. But Saul tried to destroy the church; going from house to house, he dragged out the believers, both men and women, and threw them into jail. The believers who were scattered went everywhere, preaching the message.*

Stephen's death was a terrible shock for the Church—they lost someone they loved deeply. His friends were grief-stricken. But being Christians didn't stop them from mourning the loss of their friend. Their 'loud cries' show the anguish they felt. They also show that being a Christian doesn't stop you feeling the pain of a friend or relative dying. Devout people, those who know God well, can tell God about the sorrow they feel. They don't have to pretend everything's all right.

Meanwhile, Saul tried to destroy the Church. He was very thorough. It looked like he would succeed. But he was unaware of just how strong the Church was. Strong, not because the Christians were all amazing, powerful people. No. Strong because it was God's Church—*he* stood behind it. So no matter how hard Paul tried, he would never be able to wipe out the Church.

In fact, God was using the cruel things that Saul did to make the Church stronger and bigger. The Christians who Saul chased out of Jerusalem went out into the neighbouring areas. And what did they do there? They took the good news about Jesus with them! Jesus had told the disciples that they would stand up for him in the countries around them (Acts 1:8). Little did they know that God would make use of Saul's violent persecution to help this happen. It shows that God can bring good out of even the most tragic circumstances. He is in control.

Imagine you are one of the disciples who has been thrown into jail. Write a prayer asking for God's help.

Dear farther please help all the christ-ians to have faith and help Saul because he does not know what he is doing.

4

Saul was like a wild animal hunting down its supper. He wanted to rip apart the growing band of Jesus' followers. He'd done a good job in the capital Jerusalem. So he decided to race off to Damascus, another large city where many of the frightened disciples had hidden. He was determined to track each one down and make them suffer.

Read Acts 9:3–8

As Saul was coming near the city of Damascus, suddenly a light from the sky flashed round him. He fell to the ground and heard a voice saying to him, 'Saul, Saul! Why do you persecute me?' 'Who are you, Lord?' he asked. 'I am Jesus, whom you persecute,' the voice said. 'But get up and go into the city, where you will be told what you must do.' The men who were travelling with Saul had stopped, not saying a word; they heard the voice but could not see anyone. Saul got up from the ground and opened his eyes, but could not see a thing. So they took him by the hand and led him into Damascus.

Jesus had found Saul. Just when Saul thought that he'd cornered the last few people who dared to say that Jesus was alive. Saul had expected to track down Jesus' die-hard supporters. Instead, Jesus tracked him down and showed him how seriously wrong he had been.

For a start, Saul had thought Jesus was an impostor who deserved to be killed. Now he knew better. Stephen and the other disciples had been right; Jesus was alive. Jesus had compared himself to a shepherd who goes off to look for lost sheep. (Look at Luke 15:4—'shepherd' was one of the pictures used for God in the Old Testament.) He is still doing the same job! We are able to meet Jesus because he first finds us and says, 'Here I am.' That is great news! What chance would we have if Jesus left it to us to find him?

Saul also thought that God would approve of his dragging Jesus' followers into jail. Jesus told him that by persecuting his followers, Saul was actually attacking Jesus himself. Rather than pleasing God, he was fighting against him. This was a second big surprise for Saul. Following Jesus was not thinking that he was a special person, or doing particular things. It means Jesus making an unbreakable commitment to us. A commitment so total that Jesus shared the pain of his disciples who are brutally abused by Saul. A commitment proving that God himself steps into our lives. He doesn't run away or leave us on our own.

Lord Jesus, thank you for showing me who you are. Thank you for looking me out and proving your commitment to me. Thank you for stepping into my life. Amen.

P.S. The most dangerous thing to do is to attack a Christian because it puts you in the firing line of their prayers!

That hurts!

5

Meet the

Saul spent the next few days praying and thinking about what had happened. Meanwhile . . .

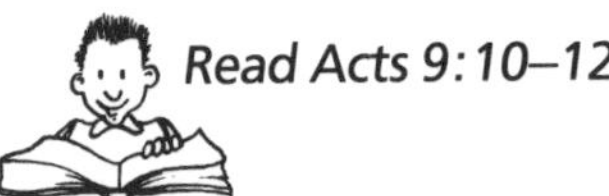

Read Acts 9:10–12

There was a believer in Damascus named Ananias. He had a vision, in which the Lord said to him, 'Ananias!' 'Here I am, Lord,' he answered. The Lord said to him, 'Get ready to go to Straight Street, and at the house of Judas ask for a man from Tarsus named Saul. He is praying, and in a vision he has seen a man named Ananias come in and place his hands on him so that he might see again.'

GO AND MEET SAUL?! – YOU MUST BE JOKING!!

How would you have answered if you were Ananias?

- ☑ Ah, Lord, if you remember right, Saul hates Christians and has come here to kill us.
- ☐ Sure, Lord, after all, Saul's a reasonable man. We've got lots in common.
- ☐ Sorry, Lord, I've no idea where Straight Street is . . .

Read Acts 9:13–15

Ananias answered, 'Lord, many people have told me about this man and about all the terrible things he has done to your people in Jerusalem. And he has come to Damascus with authority from the chief priests to arrest all who worship you.' The Lord said to him, 'Go, because I have chosen him to serve me, to make my name known to Gentiles and kings and to the people of Israel.'

Ananias must have been confused as he arrived at Straight Street. What would have been your first words to Saul if you were Ananias?

- ☐ I didn't want to come here but God told me to.
- ☑ Hello brother.
- ☐ People like you disgust me.

family

Read Acts 9:17–18

So Ananias went, entered the house where Saul was, and placed his hands on him. 'Brother Saul,' he said, 'the Lord has sent me—Jesus himself, who appeared to you on the road as you were coming here. He sent me so that you might see again and be filled with the Holy Spirit.' At once something like fish scales fell from Saul's eyes, and he was able to see again.

'Brother Saul' were probably the first words that Saul heard from a Christian after he'd met Jesus. What amazing words to hear from the friends of someone he'd helped to kill! Ananias had followed the examples of Jesus in offering love and forgiveness to an enemy. He and Saul were 'brothers' because they had both been changed by Jesus. Though there are some Christians who refuse to let God change their minds about people they hate or fear, many have learnt the same lesson.

One example is Natasha. She was a Christian living in Communist Russia. She was beaten up twice by a police squad led by a young man called Sergei Kourdakov. Her only crime was to be at a prayer meeting. She refused to hate this man for his cruelty. When he interrogated her, she told him why she believed in God. Several years later Sergei became a Christian. In a book telling his story, Sergei thanked Natasha for her kind, brave words which helped to change his life.

Sometimes we think that certain people could never be Christians. Use this prayer to pray for someone you know who seems set against Jesus.

Lord Jesus, you know and love

. . . my . . friends

Please help them to see who you are. Please help me to show them your love. Amen.

6

God's big surprise

Imagine that your most fiercesome enemy at school is the famous BIG BRENDA! She's a foot taller than you, has steel toe-caps, and scares everyone that you know (including the headteacher!). BIG BRENDA takes a special interest in you by stealing all the food and money you bring to school, and punching you when she feels like it. And whether you're nice to her, or tell her to get stuffed, she won't leave you alone.

One day BIG BRENDA comes into school with an extra large smile on her face. She offers you a sweet. She's polite. She apologizes for treating you badly. Something revolutionary has happened to her! The headline in the school newspaper might read: BIG BRENDA GETS A BIG HEART!

Saul had been on his way to Damascus. The chief priests in Jerusalem had authorized him to arrest any Christians he could find (Acts 9:2). But meeting Jesus changed everything. He still went to the synagogue in Damascus, as he'd planned. But his message changed!

Read Acts 9:20–21

He went straight to the synagogues and began to preach that Jesus was the Son of God. All who heard him were amazed and asked, 'Isn't he the one who in Jerusalem was killing those who worship that man Jesus? And didn't he come here for the very purpose of arresting these people and taking them back to the chief priests?'

The Christians in Damascus couldn't believe their ears when they heard Saul preaching about Jesus. It was completely out of character! He'd been famous for hunting down Christians. Now he was doing everything he could to speak out for Jesus. God's big surprise had given Saul a change of heart.

Write a headline for the *Damascus Daily* describing the change in Saul:

Saul is now believ

6

You may not have hated Christians or beat them up before you decided to follow Jesus. That doesn't matter! What does matter is that you've asked God to be in charge of your life. It doesn't make you a better Christian if you've got loads of spectacular crimes to confess from the past. Everyone needs God's change of heart, however well or badly they've behaved. The good news is that God is ready to accept anyone who knows they need to start again.

Almighty God, thank you for turning Saul's life around. Thank you that you've done the same for me. Amen.

Members only?

The notice outside the main part of the temple in Jerusalem made it clear. There was an outside section open to everybody. But only Jews were allowed past a certain point. Anyone else would be put to death. Anyone else was a 'Gentile'.

Many Jews thought that because God had looked after them in the past this made them better than everyone else.

Saul's first thoughts when he became a Christian were for his own people, the Jews. They thought they knew God well! But like him, they failed to recognize Jesus as God's Son. Saul thought that because he was a high-profile Christian-basher, people in Jerusalem would listen to his story. As he walked into the temple to pray, he probably passed the sign forbidding entry to 'Gentiles'. But that was the key to God's plan for him. As he prayed, God spoke to him in a vision:

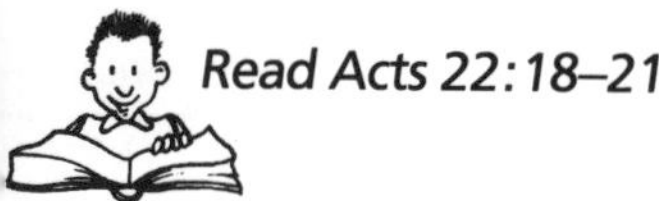

Read Acts 22:18–21

'Hurry and leave Jerusalem quickly, because the people here will not accept your witness about me.' 'Lord,' [Saul] answered, 'they know very well that I went to the synagogues and arrested and beat those who believe in you. And when your witness Stephen was put to death, I myself was there, approving of his murder and taking care of the cloaks of his murderers.' 'Go,' the Lord said to me, 'for I will send you far away to the Gentiles.'

Saul's gut feeling was that God was only interested in his own people, the Jews. People of other religions and races didn't seem that important to him. This same feeling of wanting to shut out people who are different still exists all around the world. Even when those people live in the same street or town. It often goes hand in hand with wanting to be kind to people who are the same as you.

By sending Saul to the 'Gentiles', God taught him a vital lesson. The good news about Jesus was not for a limited audience. It could not be hogged by a privileged few. It was for the whole world. It showed that God took no notice of what people look like or where they come from. Boundaries of nationality, colour or race no longer made a difference.

Are there young people in your school who are mocked because of their colour or background? How much do you go along with making fun of them?

Never				Sometimes					A lot
1	2	3	4	5	6	7	8	9	10

Father, thank you that the good news of forgiveness is for the whole world. Please use me to show other people this is true. Amen.

Quite a few young people have experienced the 'occult' with friends at school or at the local youth club. Which of these, if any, have you had contact with?

- ☐ ouija boards
- ☐ levitation
- ☐ seances
- ☐ tarot cards

One of the first places that Saul went was Cyprus:

Read Acts 13:6–12

. . .they met a certain magician named Bar-Jesus, a Jew who claimed to be a prophet. He was a friend of the governor of the island, Sergius Paulus, who was an intelligent man. The governor called Barnabas and Saul before him because he wanted to hear the word of God. But they were opposed by the magician Elymas (that is his name in Greek), who tried to turn the governor away from the faith. Then Saul—also known as Paul—was filled with the Holy Spirit; he looked straight at the magician and said; 'You son of the Devil! You are the enemy of everything that is good. You are full of all kinds of evil tricks, and you always keep trying to turn the Lord's truths into lies! The Lord's hand will come down on you now; you will be blind and will not see the light of day for a time.' At once Elymas felt a dark mist cover his eyes, and he walked about trying to find someone to lead him by the hand. When the governor saw what had happened, he believed; for he was greatly amazed at the teaching about the Lord.*

Elymas was involved in the occult. This was like being kept in a dark room, or having a blanket smothering him. It stopped him from seeing the truth about God. Paul's words sound harsh but they are true.

The 'evil tricks' that he practised may have seemed harmless enough. That's what a lot of people think about ouija boards and seances. But they close our lives to God and open us to evil spiritual forces. The result can be frightening and damage not only our relationship with God but also with our family and friends.

God made Elymas blind for a while to show just how much he was in the dark. This had a big effect on Sergius Paulus—it convinced him that what Paul had said about God was true. And it may have changed Elymas. Like Paul, his time of physical blindness may have shocked him into seeing how much he needed the light of God's truth. Luke doesn't tell us.

Who turned out the lights?

8

Almighty Father, thank you for lighting up the world through Jesus. Please help more people to see your light and accept it. Amen.

P.S. If you have been scared by taking part in seances or using ouija boards, talk about it with your minister or youth leader. Whenever you feel frightened by evil, call quietly on the name of Jesus.

** Luke, who wrote Acts, knew Saul. He uses two names for him, Saul and Paul. Saul for the first half of Acts, the start of his Christian life. Then Paul, short for Paulus, which was his Roman name. He was known as 'Paul' on his preaching travels. It was a name people he met would find easier to use.*

Paul and Barnabas travelled on, preaching about Jesus. They came to a town called Lystra, where they met a lame man. With God's power, they healed him. But . . .

Read Acts 14:11–15

When the crowds saw what Paul had done, they started shouting in their own . . . language, 'The gods have become like men and have come down to us!' They gave Barnabas the name Zeus, and Paul the name Hermes, because he was the chief speaker. The priest of the god Zeus, whose temple stood just outside the town, brought bulls and flowers to the gate, for he and the crowds wanted to offer sacrifices to the apostles. When Barnabas and Paul heard what they were about to do, they tore their clothes and ran into the middle of the crowd, shouting, 'Why are you doing this? We ourselves are only human beings like you! We are here to announce the Good News, to turn you away from these worthless things to the living God, who made heaven, earth, sea, and all that is in them.'

The Lord's Prayer has the phrase 'hallowed be your name', which means 'may people honour you'.

The confusing scene that followed the healing of the lame man left Paul and Barnabas with a difficult choice. Should they honour God?

First, they could accept the flattering attention of the people who thought they were superheroes! They could have a nice big theme park named after them and never work again.

Secondly, they could offend the crowd by telling them they'd got it wrong. The truth was Paul and Barnabas were normal people. God healed the lame man. They were just his messengers.

They chose to honour God. Not take the glory for themselves. Now, lots of people have heroes. It's natural. As we grow away from our parents, we often find other people that we look up to and admire.

Think of one of your heroes

Jesus........................

What makes them so special?

he is the son of God and he died for me.

Putting God

There's always a danger that we'll take our heroes too seriously, like the crowd in the story. It's easy to forget our heroes are human too; they make mistakes, and let other people down. We can be terribly disappointed when they let us down. Or angry that they're not what we wanted them to be. However great a person seems to be, they should never get in the way of us trusting God.

Dear Father, thank you for the people I can look up to. Thank you for all the good things about them. Please help me to remember that, like me, they're not perfect. Amen.

first

10 FREE

Imagine you work in a prison. Each night as you lock up the cells, one particular prisoner, Herbert, tells you how much he hates prison life. He can't stand the loneliness. He gets scared in the confined spaces. He's bored. Then the day of Herbert's release comes. Of all the prisoners, you know he'll be the happiest to get out. It's all he had to look forward to. He almost skips out of the front gate.

Then, two weeks later, in the middle of the night, you hear frantic banging on the gate. 'Let me in! Let me in!' It's Herbert, begging to be let back in! What would you say?

- ☐ Hah, I knew you'd miss this place. Welcome back!
- ☑ Herbert, I thought you wanted to be free?
- ☐ Keep the noise down, you'll wake everyone up!

Paul helped lots of people become Christians. He used to write letters to them to encourage them to keep following Jesus.

He was worried because he'd heard that some of them had gone back to their old religions. They thought that keeping special laws and doing certain things would make them better Christians. Paul thought that this was like trying to get back into prison, doing the things they used to hate:

Read Galatians 5:1

> *Freedom is what we have—Christ has set us free! Stand, then, as free people, and do not allow yourselves to become slaves again.*

People thought you had to be religious to get close to God. Jesus set them free

D O M !

from all that. All you needed was God's forgiveness.

Sometimes as Christians we undo the freedom Jesus gives us and tie ourselves up in chains. Chains of:

- ▷ **Pretence**—pretending that we're perfect and know everything
- ▷ **Longing**—for a perfect body
- ▷ **Boasting**—about things we haven't done or shouldn't have done.

Have you tied yourself up in any of these chains? Pray for God to make you free:

Father, you know how easy it is for me to get tied up with things that take my eyes off Jesus. Thank you that he died to bring me freedom. Please make me free. Amen.

11 Health

Which of the following is the sign of a growing Christian?

- ☐ Muscley arms
- ☐ Big feet
- ☐ Mega brain
- ☐ Strong shoulders
- ☐ Good sense of smell

Martin Luther, a famous Christian a few hundred years ago, said that Christians should develop strong shoulders. Not to look butch or get into body building. Their strong shoulders would be useful to help other people. He had in mind some advice Paul gave later on in his letter to the new Christians in Galatia:

Read Galatians 6:2

> *Help carry one another's burdens, and in this way you will obey the law of Christ.*

Paul knew that everyone has 'burdens'. That is, things that get them down. Like finding it hard to get on with parents and brothers and sisters, sadness at the death of a friend or relative, failing an exam, or being ill.

check!

11

There are two ways to deal with these problems.

One is to concentrate just on what gets us down. There can be so much that there's no time to worry about anyone else.

The second is to help share the problems of our friends. It might involve just listening to what they've got to say. It might be sticking by them through a time when they're unpopular, doing badly at school, or they're down.

Paul says that this is the only way to get on with other people because it's what Jesus did. That's why he calls it the 'law of Christ'. It sums up the way Jesus treated the people he knew, and what he said about the Jewish Law (look at Matthew 22:37–39).

Think about some of the burdens that your friends and family have. Write some of them down on the sacks and boxes the figures on the page are carrying.

Then think how you could help them carry their burden. Use this prayer:

Loving Father, I thank you for the way Jesus loved other people. Please give me strong shoulders to share the troubles of my friends and family. Amen.

12

When things go wrong

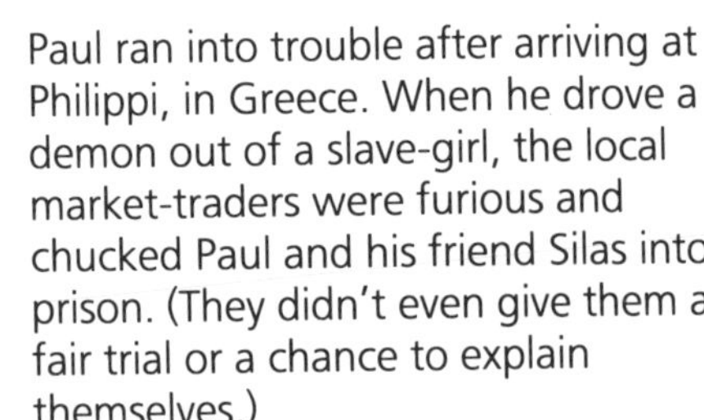

Paul ran into trouble after arriving at Philippi, in Greece. When he drove a demon out of a slave-girl, the local market-traders were furious and chucked Paul and his friend Silas into prison. (They didn't even give them a fair trial or a chance to explain themselves.)

Read Acts 16:25–33

About midnight Paul and Silas were praying and singing hymns to God, and the other prisoners were listening to them. Suddenly there was a violent earthquake, which shook the prison to its foundations. At once all the doors opened, and the chains fell off the prisoners. The jailer woke up, and when he saw the prison doors open, he thought that the prisoners had escaped; so he pulled out his sword and was about to kill himself. But Paul shouted at the top of his voice, 'Don't harm yourself! We are all here!' The jailer called for a light, rushed in, and fell trembling at the feet of Paul and Silas. Then he led them out and asked, 'Sirs, what must I do to be saved?' They answered, 'Believe in the Lord Jesus, and you will be saved—you and your family.' . . . At that very hour of the night the jailer took them and washed their wounds; and he and all his family were baptized at once.

Notice how Paul and Silas reacted to being thrown into prison. They had plenty to be cheesed off about. They'd just been whipped. They were locked in the bottom of a foreign prison. They'd no idea when they would be let out.

Instead of letting this get on top of them, they spent their time *praying and singing hymns to God.* Now this doesn't mean they were overjoyed to be locked up unfairly. It does mean that despite the cruel things done to them, they could still praise God. They knew he was in control. They knew that every situation they got into gave them the opportunity to speak out for Jesus. And that's what happened! They shared the good news about Jesus with the jailer, the man who'd put them in the dingiest cell in the prison. The jailer and his whole family became Christians!

It's easy to give up on God when things go wrong. Paul and Silas show that it's better to keep on talking to God. Some of the Psalms in the Old Testament were written by people in terrible trouble or danger. Although they're scared or angry, they can still praise God.

Read Psalm 66:1–12

Read verses 10–12 again:

You have put us to the test, God,
as silver is purified by fire,
so you have tested us.
You let us fall into a trap
and place heavy burdens on our backs.
You let our enemies trample over us;
we went through fire and flood,
but now you have brought us to a
place of safety.

Tell God about the things you are finding difficult. Then use verse 20 as you pray.

I praise God,
because he did not reject my prayer
or keep back his constant love from me.

13

I can't

13

Paul continued his preaching tour around Greece. As he got ready to go to Corinth, a busy city famous for its big business and racy living, he was worried. Later, when he wrote to the young Christians in Corinth, he told them why . . .

Read 1 Corinthians 2:3

> *. . . when I came to you, I was weak and trembled all over with fear . . .*

He was worried because he knew that his message about Jesus would be unpopular in Corinth. He wanted to speak out for Jesus. But he feared that people wouldn't listen to what he said. They'd make fun of him for being different, for daring to say that Jesus was the Son of God. They'd think he was stupid. They'd never believe his message that Jesus rose from the dead. They'd probably have a go at him for saying that they needed God's forgiveness for things they'd done wrong.

Paul's fears might seem familiar. At school or at home it can be just as hard to believe things that others disagree with. It can be terrifying to say out loud things you know are true about Jesus.

Paul could have avoided trouble by dressing up his message in fancy words. Or leaving out the bits people wouldn't like. He didn't. Instead . . .

> *. . . while I was with you, I made up my mind to forget everything except Jesus Christ and especially his death on the cross.*
>
> 1 Corinthians 2:2

This meant speaking clearly about Jesus' death on the cross. It meant trusting that God would use what he said to point people to Jesus, however nervous or stupid he felt.

Here's a list of fears that people have about sharing their faith in Jesus. Number them from 1 to 5 to show which are most frightening for you (1 for the most difficult):

...... being called stupid
...... not knowing what to say
...... being called a spoil-sport
...... losing friends
...... afraid of letting God down

Almighty God, you know that sometimes I'm scared about speaking out for Jesus. Thank you that I don't have to be an amazing speaker and have all the answers. Please use my weak efforts to tell other people about you. Amen.

14

Imagine you get seats for a World Cup football match; Brazil against your country's team. You find yourself sitting with the Brazilian fans. They all cheer wildly as the teams kick off. But after about ten minutes, one of the Brazilian fans starts shouting for his own local football club. Another shouts for hers. Soon they've all stopped watching the football. Instead, they're fighting over whose home team is best!

Paul faced a situation like this with his new Christian friends at Corinth. After his time with them, the church started to split up. Each group had a particular church leader as its hero. And soon they started to argue. (You can imagine that at an English football match the Manchester United and Arsenal fans might start arguing as well!)

Read 1 Corinthians 1:10–13

By the authority of our Lord Jesus Christ I appeal to all of you, my brothers and sisters, to agree in what you say, so that there will be no divisions among you. Be completely united, with only one thought and one purpose. For some people from Chloe's family have told me quite plainly, my friends, that there are quarrels among you. Let me put it this way: each one of you says something different. One says, 'I follow Paul'; another 'I follow Apollos'; another, 'I follow Peter'; and another, 'I follow Christ'. Christ has been divided into groups! Was it Paul who died on the cross for you? Where you baptized as Paul's disciples?

The same things happen in any church or youth group. There's a danger of latching on to individuals and thinking they're the only people to be like. Some might go for the minister because he's so holy. Some might go for the youth leader because she's so cool. Others might go for someone who helps with the music because they're so funny.

Paul's not against respecting other Christians. But he does tell his friends at Corinth to remember that they are *Christ*ians—people whom Jesus Christ has set free. Knowing that will stop them swapping Jesus for someone else, however good they are. It will help them be 'Christians United'.

1. Think about those who are really popular in your church or youth group. Write 3 reasons for their popularity:

Carlos..........................

Rosana..........................

Ray..........................

2. Thank God for them, and the gifts they bring to the church.

3. Pray that the church would be 'Christians United', working together for Jesus.

14

Christians United!

15

Imagine you're given an antique gold coin for your birthday. Which of these would you keep it in?

- ☐ a bank
- ☐ a treasure chest with lock and key
- ☐ a special frame by your bed
- ☑ a jam jar on your bookcase

Paul wrote a second letter for his Christian friends in Corinth. He wanted them to understand what a privilege it is to be a Christian.

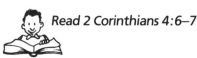

Read 2 Corinthians 4:6–7

The God who said, 'Out of darkness the light shall shine!' is the same God who made his light shine in our hearts, to bring us the knowledge of God's glory shining in the face of Christ. Yet we who have this spiritual treasure are like common clay pots, in order to show that the supreme power belongs to God, not to us.

The Corinthians were used to keeping oil or wine in clay jars. Just like we keep jam in jam jars! That's what they're for! Paul used this everyday example to remind them about two vital things about being a Christian.

First, knowing Jesus is like being given something really valuable. Paul calls it spiritual treasure. It's treasure because it shows us how to get to know God and be the people he wants us to be. Nothing is more valuable!

Secondly, Christians are like clay jars. That is, they're not the normal or proper places to keep treasure. There is nothing specially good or important about them. Nothing making them an obvious place to store something priceless. It's a brilliant picture of how Christians are ordinary people with an extraordinary knowledge of God—all because of Jesus.

You can decide to accept or reject it, but you can do nothing to make yourself worthy of God's gift.

Loving Father, thank you for this reminder that you have given me a priceless gift. Thank you for the privilege of being your child. Amen.

Hidden Treasure

16

Help!

You'd think someone was crazy if they refused an offer of help seconds before the plunged over a huge waterfall. They could be too stupid to realize the trouble they're in. Or they've got an unrealistic idea of their ability to get by. Either way they won't get far.

Paul knew all about being in dangerous situations. He told the Corinthian Christians some of the tricky spots he'd been in. (Look at 2 Corinthians 11:23–27—sounds like Indiana Jones!) Paul also had some long-standing illness or disability. He doesn't say exactly what it was (2 Corinthians 12:7), just that it was like a thorn sticking in a finger—painful and irritating. He told the Corinthians this had taught him an invaluable lesson about following Jesus:

Read 2 Corinthians 12:9–10

'My grace is all you need, for my power is greatest when you are weak.' I am most happy, then, to be proud of my weaknesses, in order to feel the protection of Christ's power over me. I am content with weaknesses, insults, hardships, persecutions, and difficulties for Christ's sake. For when I am weak, then I am strong.

Paul had learnt that the more we admit our weakness to God, the more he's able to help us. That's why Paul could say he was proud of his weaknesses. It sounds such a stupid thing to say! He could be proud of them because they gave him the chance to trust in God's strength even more. They stopped him pretending that he could get by on his own, without God.

There are bound to be times when you feel weak and in need of God's help. (It could be in your family, surviving at school, dealing with a particular temptation, worrying about what you look like.) Facing up to these things can feel like staring across a ravine with only a tiny plank to get you across. You think you'll never make it!

1. Write in the ravine one or two areas where you feel especially weak.

2. Ask God for his help. Thank him that when I am weak, then I am strong.

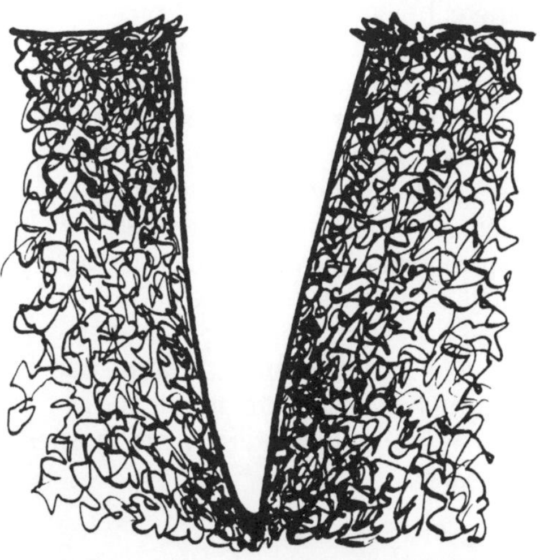

17

Most news on the radio and TV is bad. Nobody takes too much notice. Think up a good news headline that would make your friends sit up and listen:

Paul went back to see his friends in Corinth a few years later. While he was there, he wrote a letter to Christians in Rome, the capital of the Roman Empire. He wanted to visit them. They could help him get to Spain, where he hoped to carry on preaching about Jesus. But first, he must go to Jerusalem. Christians there were starving in a bad drought, and many of Paul's churches in Greece and Galatia had given him money to help them.

Paul told the Romans that he had 'good news' to share about God. (That's what the English word 'gospel' means.)

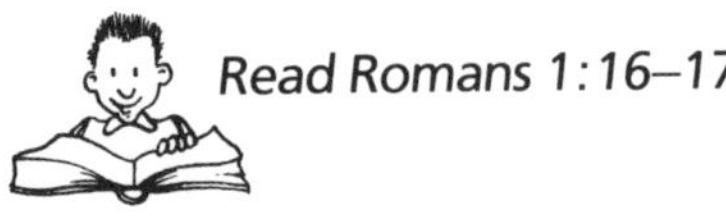

Read Romans 1:16–17

> *I have complete confidence in the gospel; it is God's power to save all who believe, first the Jews and also the Gentiles. For the gospel reveals how God puts people right with himself; it is through faith from beginning to end. As the scripture says, 'The person who is put right with God through faith shall live.'*

The Christian message is 'good news' because it tells us how powerful God is. Paul says it can 'save' people: from the evil things they've done, from living under a cloud of guilt and fear. It shows us how we can get right with God. And it's for everybody. It doesn't matter who you are. Paul had learnt soon after he became a Christian that God doesn't show favouritism. After all, he'd chosen Paul, a vicious persecutor of the Church, as one of his messengers. He wants everyone to be saved!

Lastly, it's good news because it's free. It doesn't cost you anything (although it cost God the death of Jesus). In fact, you couldn't buy it if you tried.

Which of these headlines do you think the Roman Christians should have used?

☐ Famous Christian to visit Rome!
☐ Anyone can get right with God!

GOOD NEWS

Almighty God, I thank you that your good news is for everyone. Thank you for showing it to me. Amen.

18

Sorry, I dropped off

Think of a sermon or Christian talk you've heard recently. What do you remember about it?

. . . .

. . . .

From 1–10, how would you score it for:

Length

Too short				Just right					Too long
1	2	3	4	5	6	7	8	9	10

Being easy to understand

Too simple			Just right			Too complicated			
1	2	3	4	5	6	7	8	9	10

Helping you live as a Christian

Not at all				Quite a lot					A lot
1	2	3	4	5	6	7	8	9	10

Helping you understand the Bible

Not at all				Quite a lot					A lot
1	2	3	4	5	6	7	8	9	10

Tick this box if you've ever found yourself falling asleep during a sermon or talk: ☐

One evening, when Paul was giving a goodbye sermon to Christian friends in Troas, a teenager called Eutychus was struggling to stay awake . . .

Read Acts 20:7–12

Paul spoke to the people and kept on speaking until midnight, since he was going to leave the next day. Many lamps were burning in the upstairs room where we were meeting. A young man named Eutychus was sitting in the window, and as Paul kept on talking, Eutychus got sleepier and sleepier, until he finally went sound asleep and fell from the third story to the ground. When they picked him up, he was dead. But Paul went down and threw himself on him and hugged him. 'Don't worry,' he said, 'he is still alive!' Then he went back upstairs, broke bread, and ate. After talking with them for a long time, even until sunrise, Paul left. They took the young man home alive and were greatly comforted.

Eutychus had a lot to struggle with; a four hour sermon, a hot, stuffy room, and no supper. No wonder he fell asleep! (At least if we ever fall asleep in church, the furthest we can fall is the floor! Eutychus fell out the window!)

When sermons or talks aren't exactly what we want, it's easy to get annoyed or to switch off. Here are three tips to getting more out of them:

1. Read the passage from the Bible beforehand.
2. Pray for the person giving the talk. Pray that they will understand the passage or subject. Pray that they will speak with God's wisdom.
3. Pray for yourself. Pray that you will listen to what God says. Pray for his Holy Spirit to help you put it into practice.

Almighty God, thank you for the people who teach me more about you. Please give them more of your wisdom. Speak through them by your Holy Spirit. Amen.

P.S. If you have trouble understanding what people are preaching about in your church or youth group, ask them to explain what they mean!

19 You need

Paul had told the Christians in Rome that he wanted to meet them after his visit to Jerusalem. Look at Acts 20:22–23. Which of these did Paul think was waiting from him in Jerusalem?

☐ a warm welcome
☐ people ignoring his preaching
☐ trouble

The nearer he got, the surer he was that his enemies were out to get him. When he arrived in Caesarea with his small group of friends (including Dr Luke, who wrote Luke's Gospel and Acts), he met a Christian called Agabus:

Read Acts 21:10–11

We had been there for several days when a prophet named Agabus arrived from Judea. He came to us, took Paul's belt, tied up his own feet and hands with it, and said, 'This is what the Holy Spirit says: The owner of this belt will be tied up in this way by the Jews in Jerusalem, and they will hand him over to the Gentiles.'

friends

Imagine you are Luke, travelling with Paul. What would you advise him to do?

☐ Don't go to Jerusalem.
You'll be no use to God if your enemies lock you up or kill you.

☐ Go to Jerusalem.
But be prepared for trouble there.

☐ Try a disguise.
If you don't say too much, they'll never recognize you.

Predictably, Luke and Paul's other friends were worried:

Read Acts 21:12–13

> *When we heard this, we and the others there begged Paul not to go to Jerusalem.*

But Paul would not listen to their advice:

> *He answered, 'What are you doing, crying like this and breaking my heart? I am ready not only to be tied up in Jerusalem but even to die there for the sake of the Lord Jesus.'*

Now Paul was worried too. He didn't *want* to be locked up. His friends telling him not to travel to Jerusalem made it even harder for him to keep going. But Paul knew that God wanted him to go to Jerusalem. He'd already found out that following Jesus could mean fighting through difficult situations. But, because Jesus had given up his life for Paul, Paul was ready to give up his life for Jesus.

So Paul stuck to his decision. He realized God was using Agabus to prepare him for what lay ahead in Jerusalem, not to warn him away.

In all of this, his friends' help was critical. They changed their minds and decided to support his decision. They stuck by him as he continued his journey.

Think of a friend who's finding it hard to do what God wants them to do. They may be struggling to forgive someone who's hurt them. They might be giving up on church because they reckon they've got better things to do. Use this prayer for them:

Loving Father, you know that

. . . . .

is finding it hard to go your way at the moment. Please encourage him/her with your Holy Spirit. Please help me to be a loyal friend. Amen.

20

It took a week for Paul's enemies to find out he was in Jerusalem. Mark on this scale how pleased they were to see him:

Delighted		Didn't mind		Cross			Furious		
1	2	3	4	5	6	7	8	9	10

Read Acts 21:36

They were all coming after him and screaming, 'Kill him!'

Paul only escaped because some Roman soldiers managed to pluck him out of the angry crowd. However, they blamed *him* for the trouble, and locked him up, just as Agabus had said. He then appeared before the Jewish Council. Again, people got so angry that the soldiers had to step in to rescue Paul. He was shut in in the Roman fort at Jerusalem.

Paul had been ready for trouble in Jerusalem. But now his plans to visit Rome seemed ridiculous. If he was lucky, he'd stay locked up in the fort, if he was unlucky, his enemies would get hold of him and kill him. What a prospect!

Read Acts 23:11

That night the Lord stood by Paul and said, 'Don't be afraid! You have given your witness for me here in Jerusalem, and you must also do the same in Rome.'

Jesus' presence, even in the fort, must have cheered Paul up. His mission to share the good news was not over! He would still get to Rome, and have the chance to preach there. At this time of real panic, Jesus' words gave him courage to keep on going.

There are many Christians in prison today because of their faith in Jesus. This includes young people who are arrested because of their involvement with local churches. Salamat, a fourteen-year-old boy from Pakistan, was arrested and put in prison for 'blasphemy', that is, for being a Christian. He was accused of writing insulting graffiti on the wall of a local mosque, even though he couldn't write. Then he was shot in the hand after appearing in court. A friend who was with him was shot dead.

Your prayers and support are vital. They could be a real encouragement to people like Salamat, who could easily give up hope. One way to show this support is to write letters to Christians in prison, and to the authorities who put them there. These can be simple letters to let Christians know that you are thinking about them, or to ask the authorities to let them go. Write to Christian Solidarity International for more help on how to do this. Their address is: PO Box 48, Witney, Oxon, OX8 7DD.

20

Be brave

Almighty Father, please give courage and hope to Christians who are in prison for trusting in you. Amen.

P.S. Terry Waite was held hostage in Lebanon for four years. One day he received a postcard from a Christian in England. It simply said, 'We remember, we shall not forget. We shall continue to pray for you and to work for all people who are detained around the world.'

21

Paul's enemies did try to kill him (look at Acts 23:12–22). Luckily his nephew found out about the plot against him. Paul was transferred to another Roman jail in Caesarea. While he was there, he wrote to his Christian friends in Philippi to thank them for a present they'd sent him:

Philippians 1:10–12

I want you to know, my brothers and sisters, that the things that have happened to me have really helped the progress of the gospel. As a result, the whole palace guard and all the others here know that I am in prison because I am a servant of Christ. And my being in prison has given most of the brothers and sisters more confidence in the Lord, so that they grow bolder all the time to preach the message fearlessly.

Paul tells them that *the things that have happened* to him were a great help to his work for God. Find five of them in this word square:

```
I N J U S T I C E X
Q U T V S R N E P R
F R R G N O S I R P
L A E B M Q U U K T
W E A X Z K L Q P H
U F S G N I T A E B
J K L T F G S T Y W
```

1. I ....

2. B ....

3. I ....

4. F ....

5. P ....

The things which Paul referred to were a great help for two reasons. First, they gave him the chance to talk to the Roman soldiers about Jesus. They were chained to him each day! This gave Paul plenty of time to tell them how God had kept him going through hard times, and how his life had been turned around by Jesus. Sharing the good news of Jesus mattered most to Paul; this time he was chained up as he did it! So what!

Secondly, Paul's courage in prison encouraged local Christians to follow his example. It gave them more confidence to speak out for Jesus. (Imagine you're playing a team game like hockey or football. As one of your players scores a great goal, they're injured and have to go off. Their great play will inspire the rest of the team to play even better.)

21

No problem

Paul's attitude to being kept unfairly in prison gives a good example to follow. In any difficult situation (for instance if you're ill, or facing failure or rejection), this is a good question to ask: 'What chance does this give me to point to Jesus?' It might be what you say to someone, or the way you treat your friends and family. No situation is too desperate to put you out of God's reach.

Father, thank you that even being put into prison didn't stop Paul's desire to serve you. Please teach me to see that even in the darkest moments there are opportunities to serve you. Amen.

PAUL, I JUST DON'T GET IT!! FIRST YOU WANT TO KILL ALL JESUS' FOLLOWERS – NOW YOU'RE IN PRISON FOR FOLLOWING HIM YOURSELF!!

22

Dilemma

These are some common ways of saying someone has died; unscramble the words to show what they are:

22

SAPS .... away

kick the *KEUBCT* ....

FFNUS .... it

breath your *ASTL* ....

These phrases have one thing in common. They all picture death as completely final. It's the end. Once you die, that's it, there's no more.

As Paul sat in jail, he could think about the times he'd nearly been killed. He probably wondered how much longer he had to live. He told his friends in Philippi that he had mixed feelings about the prospect of dying:

Read Philippians 1:20–24

My deep desire and hope is that I shall never fail in my duty, but that at all times, and especially just now, I shall be full of courage, so that with my whole being I shall bring honour to Christ, whether I live or die. For what is life? To me, it is Christ. Death, then, will bring more. But if by continuing to live I can do more worthwhile work, then I am not sure which I should choose. I am pulled in two directions. I want very much to leave this life and be with Christ, which is a far better thing; but for your sake it is much more important that I remain alive.

Paul was torn. He loved being alive. He loved following Jesus and being his servant. But he know that death would be even better. Dying would mean *being with Christ* without the continual struggle to serve God and other people rather than himself.

One of the phrases Paul uses to describe death is *to leave this life*. It tells us a lot about how he saw death. It's likely he was thinking about camping when he said this. Death for Paul is like taking down a tent you've been camping in for a while. It's not the end, just a change for the better. Now you can move into a beautiful house that has hot showers and won't blow down in the wind!

As Christians we don't need to worry that dying will be the end of us. It won't! It will be the start of something fantastic—knowing God more fully than we can now imagine.

Heavenly Father, you know that there are some things I fear about death. I worry about the physical pain and leaving behind my family and friends. Thank you that in dying we come closer to you forever. Amen.

23

If someone said you had an 'attitude', how would you react?

Insulted				Don't mind					Honoured
1	2	3	4	5	6	7	8	9	10

It's not often a compliment: 'That girl's got a real attitude . . .'—meaning that she's rude and selfish.

But Paul told the Christians in Philippi they should have an 'attitude'. That is, a way of thinking and doing things that would mark them out as Christians. In fact, they should copy Jesus' attitude:

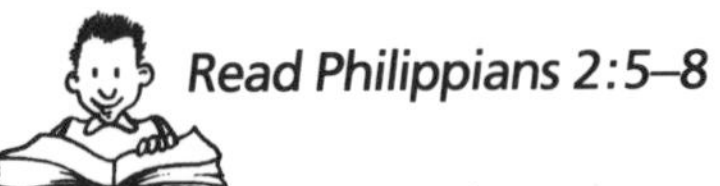

Read Philippians 2:5–8

The attitude you should have is the one that Christ Jesus had: He always had the nature of God, but he did not think that by force he should try to remain equal with God. Instead of this, of his own free will he gave up all he had, and took the nature of a servant. He became like a human being, and appeared in human likeness. He was humble and walked the path of obedience all the way to death—his death on the cross.

The words Paul uses come from a song written by the first Christians. The song celebrates Jesus' attitude to life. Jesus, who shared God's glory and power, chose to give it all up to become a human being. And he didn't come as a great king. He decided to be a servant to everyone, to give up his time and energy, and finally his life, for other people.

It is difficult to give up our time and money for other people, even the ones we love. But having this 'Jesus attitude' lets Mark choose to put himself out for others. Often it means deciding to hang out with people who are always left out at his school. He's pretty sure that Jesus would do the same, and so doesn't mind his friends calling him a sad case himself.

How would people who know you well describe your 'attitude' to life?

- ☐ fun-loving
- ☐ generous
- ☐ selfish
- ☐ enthusiastic
- ☐ ambitious
- ☐ boring
- ☐ something else . . . .

Copy Jesus

Copy Jesus

Lord Jesus, thank you for choosing to give up all you had to serve others. Please help me to have your attitude. Amen.

P.S. Try fitting the words of Paul's song to music—you could use a song that you already know and change the words.

Julius was a Roman officer working in 'The Emperor's Regiment'. His main job was to watch over the ships that transported grain from Egypt to Italy. But sometimes he took charge of prisoners sent to Rome to appear in court there. It was Julius' job to guard Paul, who, as a Roman citizen, had asked for his case to be tried in Rome.

It is possible that Julius had heard of a new group called 'Christians', but to him, Paul was just another prisoner. But by the end of their trip, Julius respected Paul so much that he saved his life! To find out why, you need to read all of Acts 27. Luckily, Dr Luke was travelling with Paul, and gives an eye-witness account of what happened.

Read Acts 27

Four things in particular must have impressed Julius:

1. Paul's wisdom (27:10)—as an experienced sailor he warned the captain that it was dangerous to sail so late in the year.
2. Paul could handle a crisis—when everyone else had given up, Paul encouraged people to keep going (27:21–22).
3. Paul was a quick thinker—he spotted the sailors trying to escape and put a stop to it (27:31).
4. Paul was practical—he got everyone to eat something before the boat ran aground (27:33–34).

Imagine Julius had to fill out a report for his commanding officer. What do you think he said about Paul?

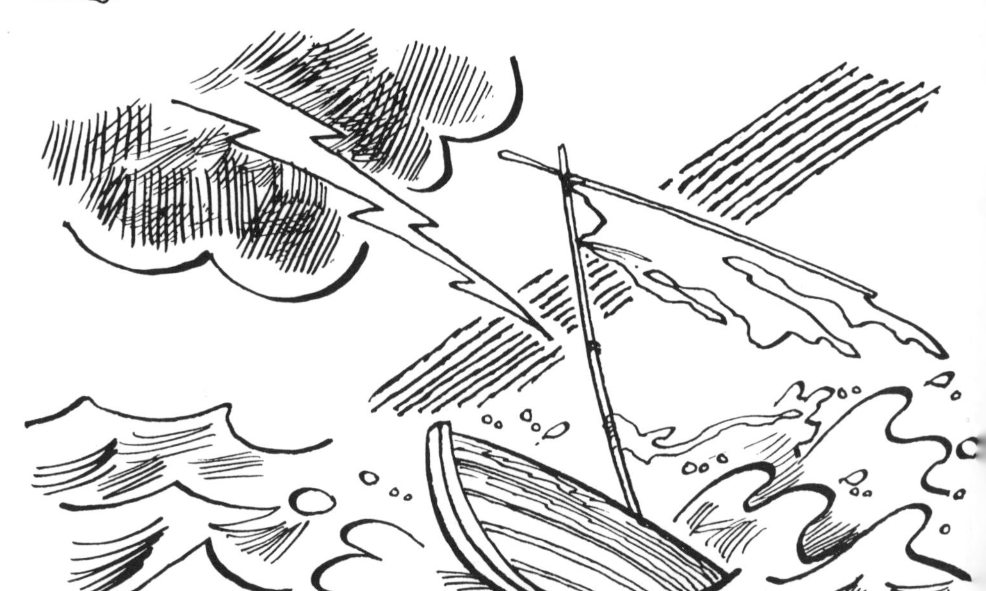

THE EMPEROR'S REGIMENT
REPORT ON VOYAGE TO ROME

THE PRISONER PAVL SVRPRISED ME MANY TIMES...

Almighty Father, thank you for making Paul the person he was. Please help be to make the most of what you've given to me. Amen.

25

How superstitious are you?
Complete the survey:

Does it bother you if someone opens an umbrella inside?

Not at all — A bit — A lot

1 2 3 4 5 6 7 8 9 10

Is it 'bad luck' to walk under a ladder?

No — A bit — Yes

1 2 3 4 5 6 7 8 9 10

How often do you read your horoscope?

Never — Once in a while — Every week

1 2 3 4 5 6 7 8 9 10

How much notice do you take of it?

None — A bit — A lot

1 2 3 4 5 6 7 8 9 10

Count up your score ....

Under 12 = not superstitious,
Over 32 = very superstitious.

The islanders that Paul and the shipwrecked crew met on Malta would have scored full marks. They were ready to believe just about anything!

Read Acts 28:2–6

The natives there were very friendly to us. It had started to rain and was cold, so they lit a fire and made us all welcome. Paul gathered up a bundle of sticks and was putting them on the fire when a snake came out on account of the heat and fastened itself on his hand. The natives saw the snake hanging on Paul's hand and said to one another, 'This man must be a murderer, but Fate will not let him live, even though he escaped from the sea.' But Paul shook the snake off into the fire without being harmed at all. They were waiting for him to swell up or suddenly fall down dead. But after waiting a long time and not seeing anything unusual happening to him, they changed their minds and said, 'He is a god!'

It's easy to make fun of these islanders for jumping to the wrong conclusions so quickly. They couldn't understand what was happening and this made them ready to believe almost anything.

But there's still a lot that's hard to understand today. Things that happen to us and our friends seem so random. It's tempting to think that horoscopes could really hold the key to happiness. They're easy to accept because they normally say what you want to hear: like there'll be people queuing up to go out with you!

There will always be things we don't understand. God knows that we worry about this. The way round it is to trust that he will stay on our side, whatever happens. Not to guess what will happen next, or rely on the advice of people who don't know us and who don't believe that God is in charge of the world. That's what Paul seems to have done, even as he shook off the dangerous snake hanging from his finger.

Malta miracle

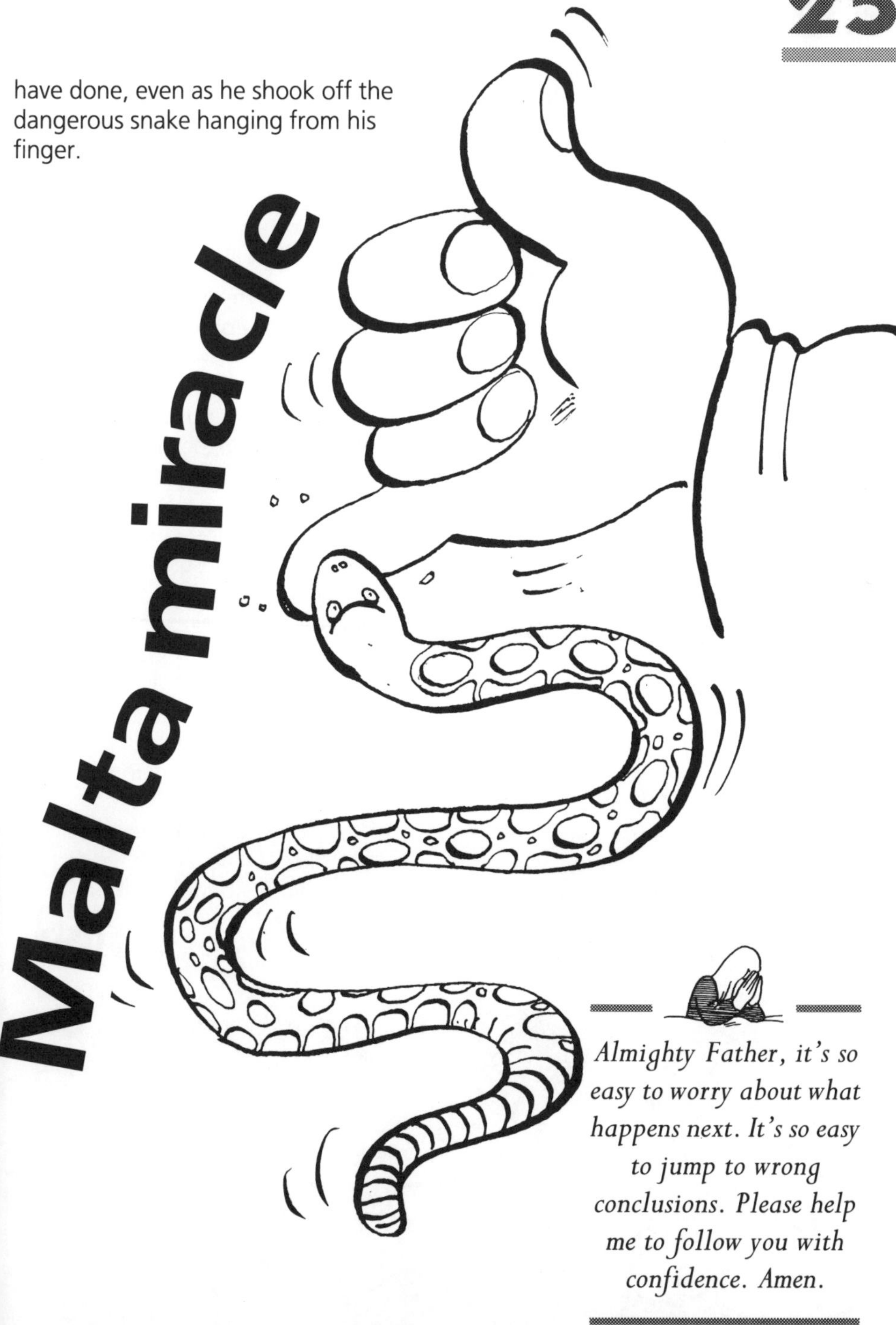

Almighty Father, it's so easy to worry about what happens next. It's so easy to jump to wrong conclusions. Please help me to follow you with confidence. Amen.

26

Paul spent three months in Malta. Then, at last, he was taken to Rome and put under house arrest there. God had kept his promise that Paul would get to Rome. But Paul hadn't expected to get there as a prisoner in chains!

Paul was determined, as always, to preach about Jesus. He contacted his fellow Jews in Rome. He wanted to convince them that Jesus had been the Saviour the Jews were waiting for, not a common criminal.

Read Acts 28:23–24, 30–31

> *So they fixed a date with Paul, and a large number of them came that day to the place where Paul was staying. From morning till night he explained to them his message about the Kingdom of God, and he tried to convince them about Jesus by quoting from the Law of Moses and the writings of the prophets. Some of them were convinced by his words, but others would not believe . . . For two years Paul lived in a place he rented for himself, and there he welcomed all who came to see him. He preached about the Kingdom of God and taught about the Lord Jesus Christ, speaking with all boldness and freedom.*

Paul knew that the Jews in Rome would have questions about Jesus. They had heard about him, and the people who followed him. But they knew almost nothing about what Jesus said and did while he was alive, or that he came back to life after being executed.

Which of these questions do your friends ask about Jesus? Tick the ones you've been asked:

- ☐ Did Jesus actually exist?
- ☐ Why did Jesus die?
- ☐ What's Jesus got to do with my life now?
- ☐ Why all the fuss about Jesus? He was just a good man with impossible dreams.
- ☐ How do I know what Jesus said and did?
- ☐ What did Jesus look like?

NYAH! NYAH!! WHIMPY CHRISTIAN!!

You may have struggled to answer these questions. Or you may be disappointed that your friends still don't believe in Jesus after all you've said. This does not mean that you've failed as a Christian.

Even Paul found it difficult to convince everyone that Christianity was true. There were plenty of people who thought he was a liar, a fanatic, or plain stupid. He knew that not everyone he talked to would leap in the air and shout 'I want to be a Christian!' But this didn't stop him doing his best to help people see the truth about Jesus. He was sure that this was the greatest sign of friendship that he could show.

Loving God, thank you for the people who first told me about you. Thank you for their concern for me. Please help everyone in my church, including me, to tell others the truth about Jesus. Amen.

ROME AT LAST

27

SEIZE ME IF I SHOULD TRY TO ESCAPE AND SEND ME BACK TO MY MASTER

If you found this tag lying on the street, who would you think it belonged to?

☐ a dog
☐ a cat
☐ a slave
☐ a hamster

In Paul's day, this tag was worn by all slaves. It reminded them that they weren't free to do as they pleased. Their master owned them as a piece of property.

While he was under house-arrest, Paul met a run-away slave called Onesimus. Onesimus soon became a Christian. As they got to know each other, Paul found out that Onesimus had run away from an old friend of his, Philemon, a Christian who'd helped Paul out in the past.

This gave Paul something to think about. By law, he should send Onesimus back to Philemon. But he and Onesimus had become great friends. And, more importantly, Onesimus was now a Christian. This made him and Philemon fellow-Christians as well as slave and master. Paul wrote a short letter to Philemon, asking him to take back Onesimus:

Read Philemon 15–16

> *It may be that Onesimus was away from you for a short time so that you might have him back for all time. And now he is not just a slave, but much more than a slave: he is a dear brother in Christ. How much he means to me! And how much he will mean to you, both as a slave and as a brother in the Lord!*

The relationship between Onesimus and Philemon changed because now they were *dear brothers in Christ*. They were now part of the same family. God's family! Being part of God's family didn't mean they looked the same, or were naturally good friends. But, as Christians, they were both set free to love each other by accepting God's forgiveness and following Jesus.

Some Christian young people in South Africa have learnt this lesson. Black, mixed race and white teenagers have refused to stay at arms-length and continue to distrust each other. They have met together to play sport, sing

A new brother

and go to the beach, to show that they are Christian brothers and sisters, despite their differences and getting grief from their family and other friends. It doesn't mean that they're immediately best friends. But it is their way of showing that they're all part of God's family.

Imagine Philemon gave Onesimus a new badge. What would it say?

Almighty God, you have made me part of your family. Thank you for the many new brothers and sisters this gives me. Help us to break down the barriers between us. Amen.

P.S. Talk to your youth leader about getting together with other young Christians near you. How could you show you're all part of the same family?

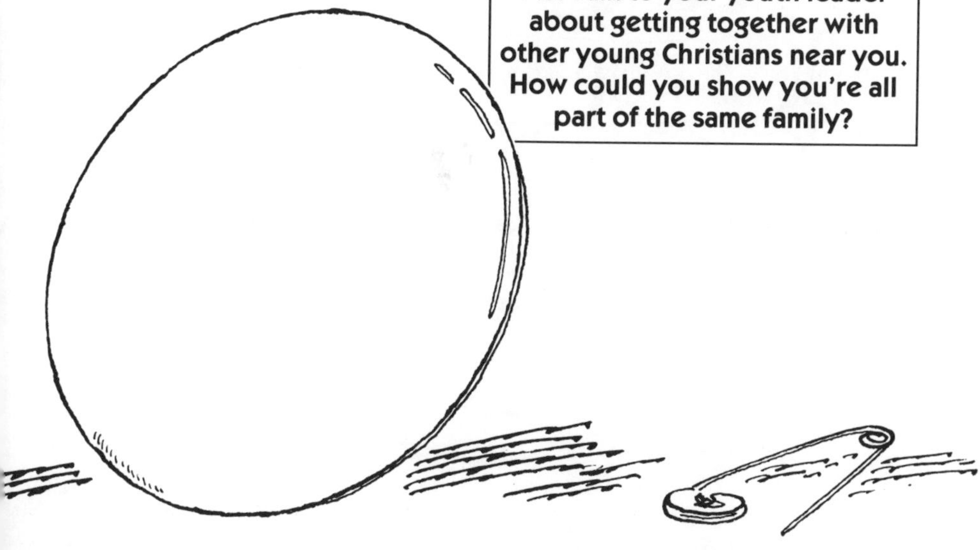

28

Write down the name of one person you know who is a leader in your church (it might be the minister or the youth leader).

. . . .

Whatever they do in the church, one thing is certain. They need your support. They may make their job look really easy. You might think that they're the last person you could help. But Paul was certain that the best way for his Christian friends to help him was to pray for him, as often as they could.

Read Colossians 4:2–4

Be persistent in prayer, and keep alert as you pray, giving thanks to God. At the same time pray also for us, so that God will give us a good opportunity to preach his message about the secret of Christ. For that is why I am now in prison. Pray, then, that I may speak, as I should, in such a way as to make it clear.

Paul could have asked them to pray for all kinds of things. He was under house-arrest and not sure when he'd get out. But his first priority was simple. He wanted to keep on speaking out for Jesus to people he met. He wanted to make the most of every opportunity he had to do this. And he knew that he needed God's help to say things in a way that people could understand.

Of course there are lots of things you can pray for the people who lead your church. Try asking them what you can pray for—it will make their day! But Paul's prayer request is a good place to start for praying for our church leaders.

Find a piece of card or paper. Write this prayer on it. Keep the card by your bed—maybe as a bookmark or stuck to your wall. When you see it, pray for the leaders of your church.

Almighty God, thank you for the leaders of my church. Thank you for the way they serve you. Please give them opportunities to speak out for you. Please give them wise words to say. Amen.

29

Keep fit

How would you expect them to get on at the next Olympics?

No chance				OK				Gold medal	
1	2	3	4	5	6	7	8	9	10

You're appointed as their new trainer. Pick out the three most important things you'd include in a programme to get them back into shape:

- ☐ 30 minutes sunbathing daily
- ☐ Regular work-out sessions
- ☐ New pair of sunglasses
- ☐ Healthy diet
- ☐ Good coaching to improve skills
- ☐ As much beer as they could drink

YESTERDAY A GROUP OF TOP-RANKING ATHLETES ANNOUNCED THEY HAD STOPPED ALL TRAINING. THEY SAID THEY WERE TIRED OF GETTING UP EARLY, ENDURING LONG WORK OUT SESSIONS, AND SAYING "NO" TO CREAM-CAKES AND DOUBLE CHOC ICE CREAM....

One of the last surviving letters that Paul wrote was to a young Christian friend called Timothy. He wanted to give Timothy some advice about his work with the local church.

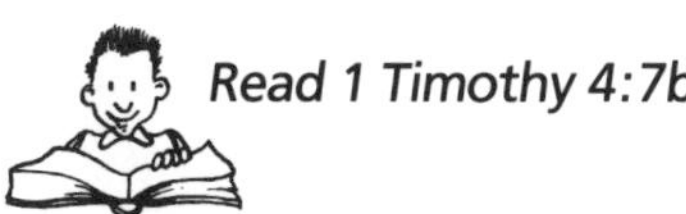

Read 1 Timothy 4:7b–8

> *Keep yourself in training for a godly life. Physical exercise has some value, but spiritual exercise is valuable in every way, because it promises life both for the present and for the future.*

Christians need to keep fit! Paul thought that physical exercise, like jogging, was a great idea. But he thought that staying fit spiritually was much more important. That doesn't mean going for a jog humming a Christian song. Or doing aerobics in a church! Paul meant giving time to building up our friendship with God and getting more like Jesus. He knew that being a Christian without doing this was as ridiculous as an athlete not bothering to train. He knew that sometimes this could be hard work, and feel repetitive. But, like an athlete getting ready for a big competition, he kept going.

Match up these three parts of a training programme with what they could mean for a Christian staying fit spiritually:

Healthy diet	**Praising God and praying for others**
Regular workout sessions	**Hearing older Christians explain how to follow Jesus**
Good coaching	**Reading the Bible (and using Bible notes to help you understand it)**

Now fill in your Weekly Spiritual Exercise Chart. It gives you the chance to plan to stay fit. Be realistic about how much time you have to spare.

	Reading the Bible	**Praying by yourself**
When?	. . . .	. . . .
How long?	. . . .	. . . .
	Learning from older Christians (in talks/sermons)	**Praising God and praying for others**
When?	. . . .	. . . .
How long?	. . . .	. . . .

Almighty God, I want to build up my relationship with you. I know how much I need your help to do this. Please make me more like Jesus. Amen.

30

Looking forward

Think about one thing you're really looking forward to doing (it might be finding the perfect job, visiting a far-away place, getting married . . .)

. . . .

Why are you so looking forward to it?

. . . .

There are lots of exciting things to dream about and plan for. That's one of the great things about living in God's world. A few weeks or months before Paul was finally executed in Rome, he looked back at his life. He thought about what had kept him going when being a Christian had been tough. One thing stood out:

Read 2 Timothy 4:6–8

As for me, the hour has come for me to be sacrificed; the time is here for me to leave this life. I have done my best in the race, I have run the full distance, and I have kept the faith. And now there is waiting for me the victory prize of being put right with God, which the Lord, the righteous Judge, will give me on the Day—and not only to me, but to all those who wait with love for him to appear.

Paul had kept going because he could be sure about the future. He knew that he could follow in Jesus' footsteps, and not be beaten by death. He was convinced that, thanks to God's forgiveness, he could enjoy living with God forever.

Dying would be like crossing the finishing line after a long-distance run. The painful struggle would be over. An amazing winner's medal would be waiting for him. It was this that Paul had been looking forward to. Especially when he was chucked in prison or let down by friends.

He wanted Timothy to be sure that the same was true for all Christians. There was nothing special about Paul that guaranteed him a place in heaven. God gives the same prize of eternal life to everyone who keeps on trusting in Jesus.

There's a lot to look forward to!

Almighty God, thank you that I can be certain of knowing you forever. The thought of dying is frightening. But I know that it will be the time when I know you better than ever. Thank you for the hope this gives me now. Amen.

What next?

The *Following Jesus* Series

If you have enjoyed using *Sent by Jesus*, you might like to look at other titles in the series. All are available singly or in packs of 10 copies.

Following Jesus—31 units which explore the basics of the Christian faith.

Serving Jesus—31 units which encourage us to serve Jesus in the world today.

Praying with Jesus—31 units which explore Jesus' teaching on prayer.

The Power of Jesus—28 units which consider the power of Jesus as seen in the seven signs in John's Gospel.

Picturing Jesus—28 units which consider the seven 'I Am' sayings in John's Gospel—the pictures which Jesus used to illustrate and show who he was: 'I am the Good Shepherd', 'I am the Vine', 'I am the Bread of Life', 'I am the Way, the Truth and the Life', 'I am the Light of the World', 'I am the Resurrection and the Life', 'I am the Gate'.

Stories by Jesus—31 units which consider ways Jesus used parables to illustrate his teaching and shows how they still relate to and challenge us 2,000 years later.

Surprised by Jesus—31 units which consider ways in which Jesus surprised people by what he said and what he did.

The Spirit of Jesus—31 units which consider the Holy Spirit: the story of the Spirit, pictures of the Spirit and the Holy Spirit and you.

The Teaching of Jesus—29 units consider the teaching of Jesus in the Sermon on the Mount (Matthew 5–7).

The Touch of Jesus—28 units which look at the impact of the transforming touch of Jesus on those he met.

The final volume in the series, *The Cross of Jesus*, is in preparation.

All titles in the series are illustrated throughout by Taffy, and are available now from all good Christian bookshops, or in case of difficulty from BRF, Peter's Way, Sandy Lane West, Oxford, OX4 5HG.

If you would like to know more about the full range of Bible reading notes and other Bible reading group study materials published by BRF, write and ask for a free catalogue.